Animal Antics

SHARKS

Copyright © ticktock Entertainment Ltd 2007
First published in Great Britain in 2007 by ticktock Media Ltd.,
Unit 2, Orchard Business Centre, North Farm Road,
Tunbridge Wells, Kent, TN2 3XF

Author: Monica Hughes
Designers: Alix Wood and Emma Randall
Editor: Rebecca Clunes

ISBN 978 1 84696 496 1 pbk

Printed in China

A CIP catalogue record for this book is available from the British Library.

Illustrations © Andrew Griffin 2001

This is Stanley.

He would like to have
a penguin for a pet.

Stanley would also like to
have these animals as pets.

pigeon

hedgehog

mice

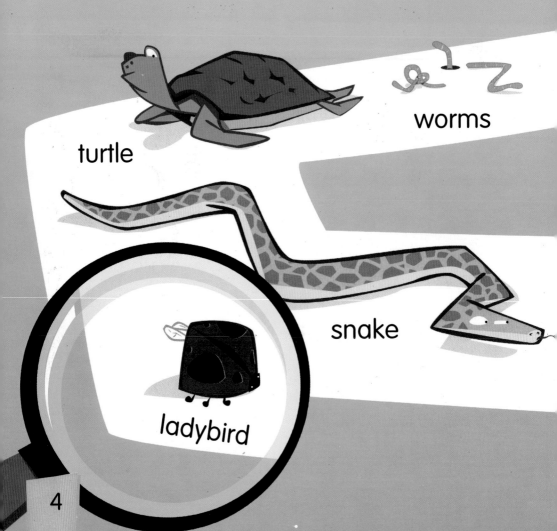

turtle

worms

snake

ladybird

budgies

dog

elephant

Stanley thinks a shark would make a good pet.

Do YOU think a shark would be a good pet?

True or False?

Some sharks are only 20 centimetres long.

Answers for True or False are on page 32.

Stanley knows a lot about sharks. He knows sharks have different kinds of fins.

dorsal fin

eyes

gill slits

nose

The fins help the shark move through the water.

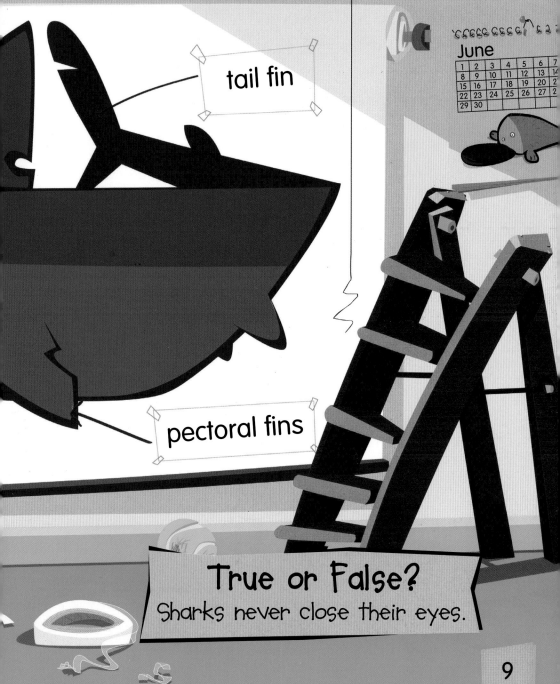

tail fin

pectoral fins

June

1	2	3	4	5	6	7
8	9	10	11	12	13	14
15	16	17	18	19	20	2
22	23	24	25	26	27	2
29	30					

True or False?
Sharks never close their eyes.

Stanley's mum thinks a goldfish would make a good pet.

Do you think Stanley would like a goldfish as a pet?

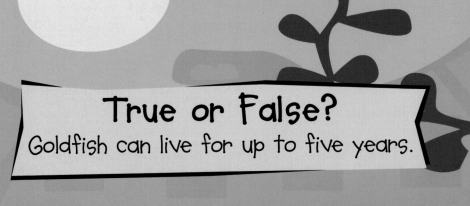

True or False?
Goldfish can live for up to five years.

Did You Know?
Goldfish were kept
as pets in China
1000 years ago.

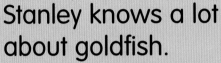

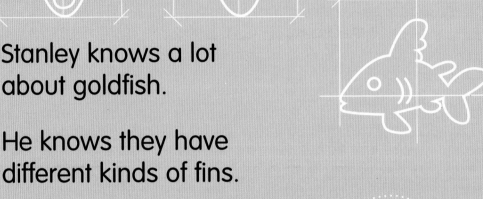

Stanley knows a lot
about goldfish.

He knows they have
different kinds of fins.

The fins help the goldfish
to swim up and down,
turn and stop.

Did You Know?

A young goldfish
is called a fry.

Sharks and goldfish need oxygen to breathe.

Their gills take oxygen from the water.

oxygen out

The water goes into their mouths.

When they close their mouths the water goes out over their gills.

True or False?
Some sharks cannot breathe unless they are swimming.

Most goldfish are very easy to see. They can be gold, white, red, **multicoloured** and even black.

Some sharks are difficult to see. Many sharks have a dark coloured back but are lighter underneath.

True or False?

Some sharks are spotted or striped.

Stanley knows that a goldfish is easy to look after.

He can get a goldfish at a pet shop.

He can take it home in a plastic bag.

A goldfish must only stay in the plastic bag for a short time.

Stanley could not get a shark
at a pet shop.

If Stanley did get a shark
how would he get it home?

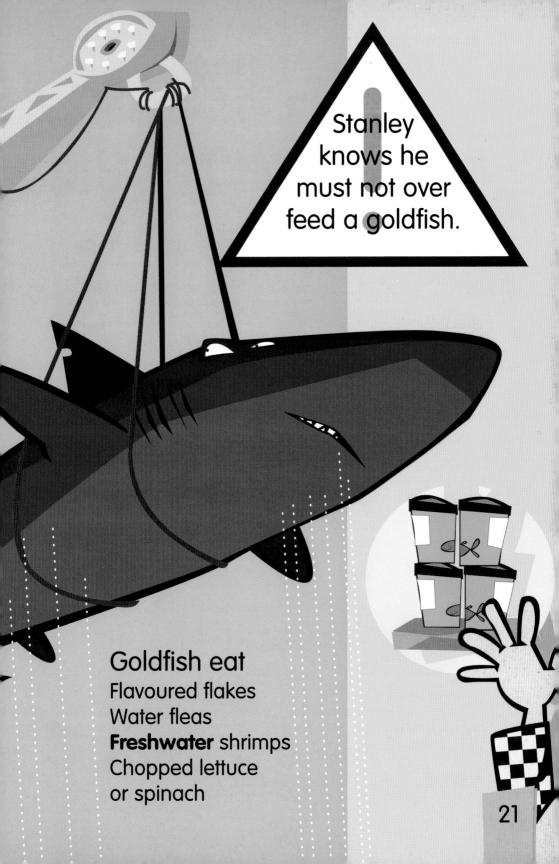

Stanley
knows he
must not over
feed a goldfish.

Goldfish eat
Flavoured flakes
Water fleas
Freshwater shrimps
Chopped lettuce
or spinach

Stanley knows that different sharks eat different kinds of food.

Some sharks eat
Fish
Seals
Penguins
Octopus
Dolphins
Eels
Squid
Other sharks

SHARK FOOD

Did You Know?
Some sharks eat only tiny sea creatures called **plankton**.

Stanley knows that most goldfish
live in **freshwater**.

He could get cold water for his goldfish from a tap.

True or False?
Most sharks live deep in the ocean.

Sharks live in the **ocean**. They like salty water.

Stanley can keep a goldfish
in an **aquarium**.

Where would he keep
a **big** shark?

He would need a
tank as big as
a house.

Did You Know?
There are more than 350 different kinds of sharks.

Stanley has his new pet and it is a goldfish!

It lives in an **aquarium** with **gravel** at the bottom.

There are plants and places for the goldfish to hide.

Stanley still likes sharks.

Now he does not want one as a pet.
He knows sharks eat goldfish!

Glossary

Aquarium   Glass tank for holding fish.

Multicoloured Many colours.

Freshwater   Water which does not have salt in it.

Gravel   Small stones.

Ocean   Very large sea.

Plankton   Tiny plants and animals eaten by fish.

True or False answers

Page 7   True

Page 9   True

Page 10   False
                Some goldfish can live
                for up to 25 years.

Page 15   True

Page 17   True

Page 25   True

Page 29   False
                Goldfish like
                to live with
                other goldfish.